serving the assembly's worship

A HANDBOOK FOR ASSISTING MINISTERS

Christian Scharen

Augsburg Fortress

SERVING THE ASSEMBLY'S WORSHIP
A Handbook for Assisting Ministers

Also available:
Leading Worship Matters: A Sourcebook for Preparing Worship Leaders
 (ISBN 978-1-4514-7806-8)
Getting the Word Out: A Handbook for Readers (ISBN 978-1-4514-7807-5)
Altar Guild and Sacristy Handbook, 4th rev. ed. (ISBN 978-1-4514-7809-9)
Worship Matters: An Introduction to Worship (Participant book ISBN 978-1-4514-3605-1;
 Leader guide ISBN 978-1-4514-3604-4)

Cover design: Laurie Ingram
Cover photo: Mark Christianson
Interior design: Ivy Palmer Skrade, Erica Rieck
Editor: Suzanne Burke

Manufactured in the U.S.A.

ISBN 978-1-4514-7808-2

17   16   15   14   2   3   4   5

Contents

Introduction

"Just as I have loved you, you also should love one another." John 13:34b

Welcome. We begin a journey together here to explore the beauty and dignity of the assisting minister role in worship. We will consider the basics of assisting in worship—the why, who, and what questions. As an assisting minister, you will find it helpful to have some biblical, theological, and historical understanding of the role. That background is provided in chapters 2 and 3. And, of course, this handbook provides guidance on specific how-to questions. You may wish to turn directly to chapter 4 where such questions are addressed—but do come back around to the "why" and "who" chapters. Those new to this crucial role will do best as assisting ministers when they have gained a basic map of the territory.

Serving as an assisting minister is much more than technique, even if posture, bearing, and bodily skill do matter a great deal. As with the presiding minister's role, the assisting minister communicates with words and actions, verbally and through body language. Taking care to understand the *reasons* for words and gestures entailed in worship leadership informs the style of presence the worship leader inhabits. As one classic book on worship leadership puts it, such study and preparation can form leaders who are "strong, loving, and wise" (Robert W. Hovda, *Strong, Loving and Wise: Presiding in Liturgy* [Liturgical Press, 1976]).

Why would an assisting minister aim to be "strong, loving, and wise" in worship leadership?

- **Strong** here does not signal the need for physical might. Rather, it refers to a grounded assurance, a proper confidence in inhabiting the role. This proper confidence arises from baptism and the gifts of the Holy Spirit, not moral (or some other sort of) superiority.

- **Loving** invites us to see that we do this worship leading in the first place simply to aid the gathered assembly in worship—whether they are lifelong Christians or first-time visitors.

- **Wise** means the practical judgment we gain over time through prayer and the Spirit's work in and through training and practice. We cannot simply jump up on a moment's notice and lead worship wisely. Instead, we grow into wisdom regarding all the subtle aspects of leading, which allow the leader to become less prominent and the thing led—prayer, scripture, song—to be central. In a word, the goal is to be transparent to the gospel.

It should be said that these three terms—strong, loving, wise—apply to the presiding minister as well. Both assisting and presiding ministers share, as in a dance of mutuality, a servant posture toward the assembly. The Holy Spirit calls worshipers to gather where God promises to be present in word and sacrament. The ministers are called out from the assembly for specific leadership roles, fostering the rhythm and pace of this encounter.

Blessings on your journey to strong, loving, and wise worship leadership for the sake of the assembly's prayer and for the sake of the world.

You are asking me?
The joys of assisting in worship

What is so joyful about serving in this role? If you are new to this role, you may experience many emotions, including anxiety! The truth is, when you open yourself to hearing a call to the role of assisting in worship, and even when you feel a deep call, the role might feel like a challenge to do well for quite some time. That is fine. But remember these three things, as well:

- First, the **authority** you stand upon is God's promise made in baptism. All ministers called to lead a particular congregation in worship stand on this same foundation. You are not alone, but held and guided by the work of the Holy Spirit present in the assembly. Be bold and say, "I am baptized, a beloved child of God!" Then step forward and lead using the gifts you have been given by the Spirit.

- Second, your task is to be a **servant** of God's proclamation of mercy and love, to communicate Christ for this people, this moment, and to facilitate the people's reception and response in prayer and praise. We do not and need not have something to say or do to make our leadership acceptable or worthy. As you offer your gifts of leadership, they are taken up and used by God to communicate God's own word in Jesus Christ.

- Third, you will **grow in confidence**. We cannot simply stand up and lead the liturgy the first time in a "strong, loving, and wise" manner (see page 6). We, and those we serve with, grow into this confidence—never a haughty confidence but always a humble one. We can inhabit this confidence so as to be transparent to the gospel of God's love.

A wise assisting minister I spoke with describes the journey of learning over time, and how it matters for partners working together to grow together:

As you get to work more with someone and you get to know their preferences—where do they want the book held, how high, do they want you to turn the pages or not, just some of those things you learn as you work with someone over time—it just makes it easier. Working at these things, talking about them beforehand, helps both assisting and presiding ministers gain confidence. They don't have to worry about me, I don't need to worry about them. We can deal with whatever else happens in the space together.

What is so helpful about this comment is how it points to the little things as fundamental. First, the little things are fundamental because learning them gradually, by *doing* them, is the only way to see and feel how the parts fit together in an interactive pattern of leadership with others. You can't—and needn't—have it all straight the first time you assist in worship. You will make mistakes, *and* you will grow in your ability. Even seasoned leaders continue to grow and learn.

Second, this learning over time allows a self-forgetting, an ease in the flow of the role, and this makes it possible for the worship leader to focus on the worshiping community, on what is next, and on whether things are going smoothly. This kind of leadership pays attention to the life of the whole, not only in worship but as the assembly's worship connects to daily life in the world. Those deeper connections are what you can bring into each part of your ministry, in and out of the worshiping assembly. Here, in the flow of worship leadership, true joy can be found, and it is not merely happiness. Rather, it is the joy of knowing you are being put to use for God's purposes, and in ways drawing upon the Spirit's gifts in you. As you find your way into this experience of servant leadership in worship, may you find blessing and joy overflowing!

Why assisting ministers?
A brief history

Let's start with an honest admission. The history of the church, on the whole, has been badly damaged by clergy taking over most of the roles of lay ministers in worship, including the proper role of the people of God gathered to worship! Clergy cannot—and should not—do everything in worship. Let's take a quick trip through church history. How have Christians understood the dignity and place of lay leadership in worship?

In the **early church**, the primary minister or priest was the assembly of believers. Christ, as the mediator of the new covenant, becomes the "great high priest" (Hebrews 4:14). By his dying, he absorbs the suffering and evil of the world and puts their powers to death. By his rising, he offers his life in the power of the Holy Spirit to all who believe. Through baptism and the power of the Spirit, disciples become Christ's body in the world, sharing his mission and ministry as "a royal priesthood" (1 Peter 2:9). Where the ancient priesthood offered literal sacrifices to God, this priesthood of all believers offers its sacrifice of praise to God in worship and its sacrifice of service in mission to the neighbor in need.

This basic pattern, present in scripture, finds solid footing in the practice of the early church. Clement of Rome, whose letter to the church in Corinth is among the oldest important Christian documents *not* incorporated into scripture, speaks of an ordered ministry serving in liturgy, noting "particular ministries laid down" both for the priesthood and for the laity ("Letter to the Corinthians," in *Worship in the Early Church: An Anthology of Historical Sources*, vol. 1, ed. Lawrence J. Johnson [Liturgical Press, 2009], 43, 196). All participate in the offering of gifts, which are then presented to God by the presider on behalf of all the saints.

Similarly, Paul's admonition in his own letter to the church in Corinth claims: "When you come together, each one has a hymn, a lesson, a revelation, a tongue, or an interpretation. Let all things be done for building up" (1 Corinthians 14:26b). From early in the church's life, the presiding minister's functions were limited to preaching and offering the prayer of thanksgiving at the table. All other aspects of worship were carried out by other ministers and by the assembly itself. Among those other ministers were seven "deacons" set apart by the twelve apostles for ministries of service. The text in Acts 6:1-6 notes the apostles' call to "prayer and to serving the word" (*te diakonia tou logou*), while the deacon's call was to "wait on [*diakonein*] tables." Both are called out of the multitude of the disciples, each for specific ministries of service, or *diakonia*, on behalf of the church's participation in the mission of God (Joseph A. Fitzmyer, *The Acts of the Apostles* [Doubleday, 1998], 346–348).

As those who served the table for the sake of the poor, deacons were a natural intermediary between the assembly's offering, the presiding minister's prayer over the offering, and the subsequent distribution of the offering to the needy. The deacon's role developed in worship leadership to include

- reading scripture,
- leading the prayers of intercession,
- receiving the offering,
- setting out bread and wine for the Lord's supper, and
- sending the assembly to go and serve the neighbor in love.

These responsibilities of the deacon in the early church may be thought of today as those that belong to assisting ministers. Both men and women were set apart for this servant role, as Paul notes when he commends "our sister Phoebe, a deacon of the church at Cenchreae" (Romans 16:1).

So, given this history, you may ask:

Liturgical scholars have taken many approaches to the history of worship leadership, and there's no consensus answer to that question. The earliest practices of Jesus' followers include references to many ways of leading worship, including the deep involvement of each member of the assembly. As the church became more organized around the roles of the *presbyter* (priest) and *episcopos* (bishop), and as sacramental questions came to the foreground, the laity's proper role in worship leadership was greatly diminished.

For example, Cyprian, a third-century priest and bishop in North Africa, imported structures of Greco-Roman social hierarchy that effectively shifted the center of Christian worship from the priesthood of all believers to the person of the priest. The common service (*diakonia*) of offering a sacrifice of praise to God gave way to the particular work of the priest offering a sacrifice to God on behalf of the people. These shifts led eventually to a long decline of lay or diaconal leadership in worship, and to the assembly becoming passive observers of priestly work on their behalf.

While the Reformation recovered a vital biblical understanding that God's grace in baptism conferred priestly status on all believers, a robust ministry of lay assisting ministers in worship did not really take wing until the liturgical reforms of the twentieth century. The Second Vatican Council (1962–1965) had wide ecumenical influence. Greater emphasis came to be placed on lay leadership, with a revival of a permanent order of deacons in both Protestant and Roman Catholic churches.

In North American Lutheranism, the preparations for the 1978 *Lutheran Book of Worship* encouraged shared leadership of worship by a variety of ministers, each called to her or his specific role, including a central partnership between presiding and assisting ministers. The unfortunate effect of centuries of atrophy—both of the active role of the priesthood of believers and of the proper lay-led roles assisting in worship—is that in many congregations worship leadership is thought to be "the pastor's job." Not so!

A good presiding minister is host at a party where there are many roles, including altar guilds, intercessors, acolytes, ushers, greeters, communion servers, cantors and musicians, readers of scripture, and those who tend technology, acoustics, and design of space.

Many congregations have found it helpful to identify and equip people to serve in a *primary* lay leadership role in worship. The assisting minister in this particular sense serves throughout the liturgy and is the most consistently visible lay leader, save perhaps the cantor or music minister. In this way, the assisting minister bears special significance in serving the assembly's prayer and praise.

A major hope for this handbook is that training laypeople for worship leadership roles will help revitalize and restore the proper ministry of the whole people of God and the shared ministry of presiding and assisting ministers as part of it. As Cyril Eastwood points out, "There are but two forms of priesthood in the New Testament—the Priesthood of Christ and the Priesthood of all Believers" (*The Priesthood of All Believers: An Examination of the Doctrine from the Reformation to the Present Day* [Epworth Press, 1960]). Baptism and its anointing with oil for the giving of the Spirit serves as a consecration and ordination into this shared priesthood. On the firm foundation of our baptismal identity, and attentive to the particular gifts of the Spirit each has been given, some are called out from the assembly for particular leadership roles.

With some sense of the "why" question answered (and more information to be found in "For further reading" on pages 59–61), we now turn to asking, "Who is the assisting minister?"

Especially if you are new to this role, or are reading this handbook in an attempt to discern a call to this ministry, you are invited to explore this question. If you are an experienced assisting minister, I hope you will find new depth and beauty in your role as you reflect on its uniqueness and dignity.

Who is the assisting minister?

The proper dignity of the role

True confession: I am not an assisting minister, but a presiding minister, an ordained pastor called to "prayer and to serving the word" as Acts 6:4 puts it. My convictions about the dignity and mutuality of my shared leadership with assisting ministers led me to this handbook project. It was clear from the start, however, this resource would be stronger with another voice alongside mine: the voice of assisting ministers. I spoke with those assisting ministers with whom I regularly lead worship, and included some of their ideas in what follows to deepen and broaden the perspective offered. Our common experience leading worship as presiding and assisting ministers deepens our ability to say who the assisting minister is and why this role, a primary assisting minister, matters for our common worship in assembly.

In many congregations "assisting minister" may mean one or more of the following: reader, communion minister, leader of intercessory prayer, and perhaps other roles as well. The congregation I attend was this way when I first began to worship there. This handbook will consistently use the term *assisting minister* in its more specific sense: a primary lay worship leader serving in a full and integral role alongside the presiding minister throughout the service, almost as a mutual dance of leadership, serving the assembly by serving each other in turn. The assisting minister need not do everything; for example, in many congregations the assisting minister is not the reader. Acolytes, musicians, additional communion servers, and many other people assist with worship leadership, each playing their role.

One assisting minister commented about her own experience serving in various lay worship leadership roles over the years. In her view, there is a responsibility for the whole service that distinguishes the primary assisting minister role from others, such as reader or communion minister, which involve defined tasks at certain points in the service. In addition to the various tasks that make up the role, as the assisting minister you have a call "to the whole" and offer leadership with your presence throughout the liturgy.

She notes that in her own development, trying out various leadership roles in worship, even from a young age, helped her discern a call to the role of assisting minister. Now her young daughters serve as communion ministers, a gift to their developing understanding of the various ways we may lead in worship. Reflecting on these many roles and her own process of discernment, she describes the fit she feels between the assisting minister role and her own gifts and call. Perhaps you too feel this fit.

The assisting minister must be capable of serving in many roles (as will be discussed in the next chapter when we turn to *how* to do this role). The dynamic of the assisting minister role is shaped by its dual responsibilities: assisting the gathered community in its worship and assisting the presiding minister in her or his leadership. It is one of the few roles offering continuity throughout the service and requires some understanding of how all the parts of worship work together as a whole.

Perhaps even more than the presider, the assisting minister symbolizes a lively connection between worship and world, between prayer and mission. One might even say, to simplify, that the center of gravity for the presiding minister is the triangle of word, table, and font, whereas the assisting minister finds a center of gravity at the intersection of word and door—where we meet the neighbor in need.

Of course, assisting ministers stand at font and table, lending their presence and voice as new Christians are born, fed, and grow strong in faith. Yet presiding ministers also "stand in" on behalf of God, proclaiming God's gospel word of promise, inviting confession and offering forgiveness, drawing the penitent deeply into waters of death and rebirth, deeply into the bread and cup of salvation, declaring God's promise and the Spirit's ongoing presence and gifts. Likewise, presiding ministers proclaim the gospel and bless people on their way as they live out their place in God's mission in the world. Yet assisting ministers, in the ancient tradition of the deacon, proclaim the word of God in prayer and scripture readings, receive the offerings of the people's labors, pray for the concerns of the church and the world, and send the assembly to "Go in peace. Remember the poor."

> The dynamic of the assisting minister role
> is shaped by its dual responsibilities: assisting
> the gathered community in its worship and
> assisting the presiding minister in her or his leadership.

As an assisting minister, you are called to a "holy presence," an awareness that you are being used, or to put it more directly, that God is at work with and through you in the midst of the assembly. It is not too much to say this holy presence is "between" the presider, assisting minister, and assembly. So while we first receive God's grace and mercy as gift, we also show it by our worship. We proclaim God's mercy and love not only with words—scripture, prayer, and song—but also through our patterned ritual action. Leaders model graceful, shared action in their work together.

Assisting ministers have sometimes spoken to me of feeling hurt by pompous presiders. For your sake, dear assisting minister, let me say it plainly: presiding ministers are not holier than others, nor are assisting ministers holier than other laypeople. They are not meant to be servants of the presiding minister, any more than the presiding minister serves the assisting minister. Each of you has a role, and the mutuality of serving one another and the assembly throughout the liturgy allows for a focus on God's presence in, with, and under our actions, moving powerfully in making of us a holy people, God's delight, sent to be that delight for all the world.

> As an assisting minister,
> you are called to a "holy presence."

We turn, in the next chapter, to the nuts and bolts of this role. What do I do? How do I do it? Yet the history and theology undergirding this role do not fade far into the background; they continue to be present, giving shape to many practical considerations as we move step by step.

What does the assisting minister do?

Getting practical

The assisting minister provides, alongside the presiding minister, a consistent presence guiding the assembly's worship, from Gathering to Sending. The fourfold movement of worship names God's work in **Gathering** many people into one body, proclaiming the gospel promise in **Word** and **Meal**, for ear and eye, and then **Sending** the gathered into the world in service to their neighbor.

It goes without saying that your leadership in such a significant role will only improve by knowing some history and theology of the liturgy alongside practice with competent teachers. While this handbook is a start, you might imagine yourself starting out (or continuing) on a journey of leadership, growing into a fullness of knowledge and skill while never assuming you have "arrived." Nothing is so off-putting as a self-satisfied and pompous leader of Christian worship! As Jesus taught us, "The greatest among you will be your servant" (Matthew 23:11).

Places for worship leaders

One of the questions about how to *do* the role of assisting minister involves where to be positioned in the worship space. The answer depends a great deal on how the worship space is arranged. In a circular or semicircular arrangement where worship leaders can clearly be seen by the assembly even when seated, it may make good sense for the presiding and assisting ministers to sit with and lead out of the assembly. In an arrangement with an up-front chancel and horizontal pews extending to the back, it will be more important for the presiding and assisting ministers to have a place—modest chairs and a place to stand in front of the chairs—where they can be seen even when seated.

Wherever you sit, the calm presence you exhibit when *not* actively leading is an important way in which you invite the assembly to pay attention to others who *are* leading at the moment. The relevant baptismal principle here is that worship leaders are called *out* of the assembly, not over or against it. Whether or not the presiding and assisting ministers take designated seating with the assembly or facing the assembly, the use of space invites deliberate movement to centers of meaning at the appropriate time: to the font for confession and forgiveness; to the reading desk or ambo for scripture reading or preaching; to the table for the meal.

Some parts of the service—greeting, praying, leading in song—can be led well standing at the chair, or by stepping out from a front pew or chair and turning to face the gathered assembly. Done in this way, the presiding and assisting ministers use space to lend deeper meaning to their actions, and the flow of the whole makes sense. To compare: if the whole service is led from the table, it is less clear how the table serves as the place where Christ meets us in bread and wine, accompanied by words of mercy and forgiveness. If the greeting and prayer of the day are led from the table, it makes the table less a place for a meal and more a magical place where holy pronouncements are made. Leading only from the table also fails to ritually distinguish between the four sections of the service: Gathering, Word, Meal, Sending. They are set next to each other in order for the assembly to hear and see, taste and know the gospel in more than one way. The table begs to be seen as the place of the meal, and not also, for example, the place of greeting and intercessions.

Whether you rise from a simple chair facing the assembly or from a front pew, the point is leading worship; it is possible to lead with grace and humility wherever you are situated. In preparation for any given service, you and the presiding minister should confer about movement and use of space, as well as how each of you will embody your role. This means, of course, walking through the service so details will be thought through ahead of time—even down to the occasions when each will hold the leaders book for the other. There is no substitute for practicing in the actual space, working through the logistics needed for the service.

Now let's walk briefly through the flow of an ordinary Sunday liturgy, noting particular aspects of the assisting minister role.

Before worship

Arrival ahead of time is an obvious benefit for all concerned. Among other things, it allows talking through the order of service, noting movement and flow. It allows checking in about any last-minute major developments in the life of the world or the congregation needing mention or having bearing on some part of the worship. Presiding and assisting ministers may elect to share a single leaders book, often specially printed and placed in an attractive three-ring binder. Sharing one book adds to the practice of mutuality in leadership. It includes everything the presiding and assisting ministers need for the service, and because it is printed just for this service, each can feel free to write notes, highlight parts, and write in corrections or other changes while talking through the service. For those using a large ritual edition of the worship book—such as *Evangelical Lutheran Worship Leaders Ritual Edition*—sticky notes work well for this purpose.

Worship leaders might pause and pray together after putting on vestments and working through any final logistics. Anyone can offer prayer; it need not be the presiding minister (some sample prayers are provided on page 58). You might pray for openness of heart to God and God's people, for each leader's role, for God's word to be heard, and for the world, to which we are sent in mission. After prayer, it may be a great aid to parish ministry to be present and available in the gathering space (sometimes called the narthex) as people arrive for worship. Usually, the ushers will also be here, and perhaps greeters, and you do not want to step on their proper roles. Contexts where an instrumental prelude and/or silence are important to the assembly's gathering call for special care in honoring those gifts while at the same time extending welcome to those who enter. Perhaps at some distance from the doors, either inside or outside the worship space, presiding and assisting ministers may mingle and greet those gathering for worship. In addition to joining into the welcome and being visible as leaders even before the start of worship, they may find this to be an important time to greet newcomers or be available to hear about recent events—good or ill—in parishioners' lives. Some of what they learn may find its way immediately into the prayers of intercession for the day.

Gathering

The Gathering section of the worship service is like an accordion: it can expand or contract depending on what the Sunday and season require. For a simple gathering, the presiding and assisting ministers might simply walk to their places and turn to face the congregation. The presiding minister then will offer the greeting and prayer of the day. Here the assisting minister accompanies the presiding minister, holding the leaders book so he or she can see the words.

An extended gathering may include a thanksgiving for baptism, a full procession during a hymn, greeting, Kyrie, canticle of praise, and prayer of the day. Here the assisting minister's role is more complex:

- Worship leaders may gather at the font to lead the thanksgiving for baptism, the assisting minister holding the leaders book.

- The thanksgiving may conclude with sprinkling of the assembly as a remembrance of baptism (*asperges*). Often both the presiding and assisting ministers will circulate to accomplish this sprinkling. Each might have a bowl of water and a small bundle of evergreen branches, or the assisting minister might hold a bowl of water for the presiding minister, who sprinkles the assembly.

- A procession might be prepared at the entrance to the worship space. The presiding and assisting ministers simply walk together, pausing (and perhaps bowing) before the table and then moving to their places for the rest of the singing.

- After the presiding minister greets the congregation, the assisting minister might lead the bids of the Kyrie ("In peace, let us pray . . .") if she or he has a good voice for chanted prayer. The assisting minister may face the assembly for this litany. Here the assisting minister might be helped by the presiding minister, who may hold the leaders book and who sings the responses with the assembly. Alternatively, a cantor, soloist, or members of the choir may sing the bids from their places, a sign that the various roles of an assisting minister may be shared among several people with various leadership gifts.

- Similarly, the assisting minister may chant the first line of the canticle of praise in musical settings that call for it.

- For the prayer of the day, which prepares the assembly to hear the word, the assisting minister may hold the leaders book.

Tips on sprinkling

While some congregations have a stainless steel sprinkler (*aspergillum*) or a small broom-like brush, others use a simple fern or pine branch that is dipped in a bowl of water and quickly swung out over the assembly. Bring the branch across the body horizontally, and then smoothly but firmly fling your arm out (as you might throw a Frisbee™), aiming above heads so the drops will fall down upon people rather than smacking them directly in the face. Bringing the branch back over your shoulder and then quickly flicking the branch toward the people (as you might throw a baseball) tends to leave most of the drops of water on the floor behind you and little on those in front of you!

Word

The Word section of the service, as one of the two primary centers of worship, is when God speaks a living Word (Jesus Christ) to us in scripture reading, preaching, and song.

Reader

The assisting minister may serve as the reader (also called a *lector*) for the first and second readings. It is a servant's role, and preparing well allows the reader to proclaim the scripture confidently so that God's word, rather than the reader's personal style, is heard. Preparation involves becoming familiar with the place of reading (reading stand, ambo) and with the method of marking the appropriate readings in the Bible or lectionary. It is crucial for the lector to understand the reading, its meaning in context, and its language (both genre and vocabulary). If in your role as assisting minister you serve as the reader, you may wish to obtain a copy of *Getting the Word Out: A Handbook for Readers* (Minneapolis: Augsburg Fortress, 2013) for more guidance on this important role (see "For further reading" on pages 59–61).

Bookbearer

If the gospel is read in the midst of the assembly, the assisting minister may move during the gospel acclamation to retrieve the Bible or lectionary book and, carrying it, lead the presiding minister to the place of reading.

Intercessor

Following the sermon, hymn of the day, and perhaps a creed, the assisting minister may lead the people in response to the proclamation of the word by praying for the world. Others might be assigned this role, especially if they have prepared the intercessions and are comfortable with leading them publicly. However, it also makes sense for the assisting minister to serve at times as the intercessor, in part to maintain continuity of leadership throughout the service. In any case, it is properly the role of lay assisting ministers, not the presiding minister, and mirrors other roles mediating between worship and world historically tended by the deacon. See "Preparing the prayers of intercession" (pp. 49–56) for guidance on writing and leading the prayers.

Let me return briefly to my conversation with assisting ministers themselves. One describes her pattern of preparing the prayers:

I have a different kind of attention during the week, paying attention to what is happening in the world, in the community, at church. Then at some point I sit down to write. My pattern for the prayers is usually pretty explicit: from the world to the person. So: world, nation, community (city and congregation), and individuals we're keeping in prayer.

This assisting minister will often offer spare bids, or topics for which the assembly is invited to pray silently. She might say, for example, "Let us pray for the peace of the nations." After a time of silence she concludes with, "Lord, in your mercy," to which the people respond, "hear our prayer." This form is accessible to most leaders of prayer, and helps avoid a number of potholes: prayers becoming mini-speeches or sermons on topics dear to the one praying, or public service announcements about goings-on in the congregation or community.

In general, longer prayers tend to hinder the assembly's ability to pray, which really requires not words piled upon words, but sparer invitations to pray with space in which to actually do so. Silence as part of the prayers—not long and awkward silence, but carefully measured and evenly paced silence—gives the assembly freedom and confidence to enter the prayers with their own concerns. Some congregations make this invitation explicit by teaching the prayer pattern and then making space for the assembly's own impromptu petitions.

My assisting minister conversation partners all spoke about the importance of gestures and embodied presence as part of their leadership. In leading the prayers of intercession and other prayers (offering prayer, prayer after communion), I encourage you to use the *orans*, an ancient posture of prayer shown in the illustration on this page. While this posture may feel awkward at first, with time it will feel natural to you. In fact, one experienced assisting minister, as soon as she started talking about the openness prayer requires, moved her arms into the *orans* position!

Orans is an ancient posture of orientation and openness toward God, vulnerability, pleading, and also joy. It is an appropriate posture for the intercessor and assisting minister to assume at other times of prayer leadership. The presiding minister might also use this posture for the prayer of the day and for giving thanks at the table. The assembly may even be encouraged to join in this posture as a symbol of their participation in the communal prayer, led by either the assisting or presiding minister.

- It is appropriate for the assisting minister to lead the intercessions from a place where the prayers can be easily heard, facing the whole assembly. The *orans* posture is appropriate for leading prayer. Thus, if a reading stand or ambo is not used, the presiding minister may hold the leaders book for the assisting minister.

- The presiding minister speaks for the whole praying assembly in a concluding commendation that, like the prayer of the day, gathers all the assembly's petitions together in faith that God will hear. Assisting ministers may wish to speak the commendation themselves, and thus create the experience of continuity throughout the prayers. Either serves the purpose of collecting all the prayers into one, and it may be less awkward in some settings for this to be done by the assisting minister.

- Greeting one another in the peace of the risen Christ provides a moment of transition to the meal. The assisting and presiding ministers may greet one another and then members of the assembly before returning to their chairs for the offering, which begins the next section of the liturgy.

Meal

In the Meal section, the second primary center of worship, God speaks to us a "visible word" (Augustine, fourth century) as we eat bread and drink wine, the body and blood of Christ. Gathered by the Holy Spirit, Christ feeds us with the gift of forgiveness and new life in the word and at table. Again, by the Spirit's interceding, we become Christ's body sent into the world for the sake of all in need.

The peace flows into the offering, an ancient practice that includes a central role for you as the assisting minister. In the time of the early church, the deacon's role, between word and world, was to take from the offering the wine and bread for the meal while setting aside other gifts to be later sent to the poor. Today the offering most often comes in the form of money, but many congregations are reviving the practice of bringing gifts of food for those in need, providing an ample basket near the altar-table to receive this offering.

Setting the table

While the ushers collect the offering, the assisting minister readies the table for communion. To highlight the central proclamation that the altar is a table, the place of a sacramental meal, it might remain empty (aside from seasonal liturgical fabric, called paraments). At the time of the meal, the assisting minister "sets the table," often placing a cloth called a corporal) flat on the top of the fair linen and near the edge of the table nearest the leaders. Historically, the corporal provided a way to catch crumbs. Today it still serves that purpose and also helps keep wine drippings off beautiful linens.

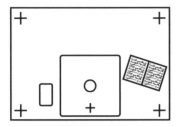

Table set with corporal, book, purificators, and one chalice, awaiting the bread and wine.

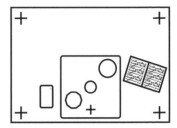

Table set, complete with bread and wine.

Receiving the offering

Once the offering has been collected and the ushers are ready, an acolyte or perhaps the assisting minister receives the offering and places it on a small credence (side) table.

Receiving and preparing the bread and wine

In some congregations, the bread and wine for communion will be carried to the table by altar guild members, communion ministers, or ushers, as part of the offering. This shows our grateful offering of the first fruits of our labor in response to all God has given. If the bread and wine are brought in procession, the assisting minister may simply receive the elements and place them on the table, centered on the cloth (corporal) just placed for this purpose. If the bread and wine have been set on a credence table, the assisting minister brings them to the table.

Some congregations have a simple plate or basket for bread and a single cup for wine, both elements left uncovered.

A vested chalice

A purificator folded in thirds lengthwise is placed over the mouth of the empty chalice.

The paten is placed on top of the purificator. (If hosts rather than a whole loaf are to be used, a large host may be placed on the paten.)

The paten is covered with the pall.

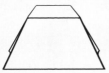

The chalice veil in the proper color of the day is placed over the pall and arranged so that a trapezoid is seen when viewed from the front.

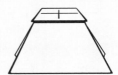

The corporal and additional purificators are placed in the burse, which matches the veil. The burse is laid on top of the vested chalice.

Others have a more formal chalice vested with a veil and burse (see illustration on this page), which when brought to the table must be opened by removing the burse, veil, and paten and setting them out on the cloth. Some congregations may have additional vessels for communion: pouring chalices for use with individual cups, or trays of individual prefilled cups. Whatever else is typically used for the logistical task of serving communion may stay on the credence table, allowing the table to clearly say *this* bread, *this* cup, given for you. It is, after all, a visible gospel word, and the clearer the image, the stronger the proclamation.

At the table

- At this point, the assisting minister stands beside the presiding minister at the table. The freestanding altar, at which the ministers face the assembly across the table, is found in many worship spaces. Where the altar is placed against the front wall of the worship space, the logistics need careful planning so that at least some of what follows—the offering prayer, the dialogue, the words of Christ's promise, for example—may be led facing the assembly.

> Some congregations use a wooden or brass book stand on the table to hold the leaders book or a ritual edition of the worship book. Alternatives include leaning the book against a less visible pillow, laying the book flat on the table, or having the assisting minister hold the book.

- The assisting minister may lead an offering prayer after the gifts have been received. Sharing a leaders book between the presiding and assisting ministers is a practice that encourages people to understand that worship is not something "done" by the clergy to be simply experienced by the assembly. Here, as elsewhere in the liturgy, the presiding minister may yield and serve by holding the leaders book as the assisting minister prays the offering prayer.

- This yielding then reverses, and the presiding minister

begins the great thanksgiving with the dialogue. The great thanksgiving is an ancient prayer paradoxically proclaiming God's saving acts, most especially in the life, death, and resurrection of Christ.

- Throughout the great thanksgiving, the assisting minister participates in several ways rehearsed ahead of time. In order to free the presiding minister to use various gestures and the orans prayer posture, handle the vessels and elements, and at suitable times make eye contact with the assembly, the assisting minister turns pages, keeps a finger on the next line in the book, leads the assembly in responses, and deftly adjusts position as the presider moves.

- The Lord's Prayer concludes the great thanksgiving, and the bread is broken for the communion.

Distribution of bread and wine

The presiding and assisting ministers may be joined at this point by additional communion ministers, and together they give the bread and wine to all who desire it. While there are no rules, the assisting minister often offers the cup alongside the presiding minister offering the bread, if there is a single station for serving communion. If there are two or more stations, the assisting minister may give the bread, and other communion ministers may serve the wine.

- To deepen the symbol of presiding and assisting ministers as servants of the assembly's worship, you may consider serving one another last.

- Following the communion, the table may be cleared, with remaining bread and wine eaten and drunk or set aside for sending to sick or homebound persons.

- Then, from the table, or after returning to a seat, the assisting minister leads the prayer after communion.

- The presiding minister may hold the leaders book so the assisting minister's arms are free to lead the prayer after communion in the *orans* posture with confidence and grace.

- This is the third transition of the service (the prayer of the day and the peace are the first two) and moves the service to its final section: the Sending.

Sending

The Sending may be simple or extended, in keeping with the character of the Gathering.

- At its most basic, the presiding minister blesses the assembly in God's name and with the sign of the holy cross, a gesture all in the assembly may make as a remembrance of baptism. As the presiding minister offers this blessing, you may lead the reception of the blessing by signing yourself.

- Following the blessing, the assisting minister sends the congregation forth with words such as "Go in peace. Serve the Lord." Similar words may be used, alternating, perhaps, by season.

- The dismissal may be delayed if the congregation uses the Sending for announcements, a sending hymn, or a recession (if a procession began the service). In some cases a brief prayer of sending for communion ministers—who are sent to carry the meal just shared to those unable to attend—will be added before the blessing and dismissal.

After worship

After worship, presiding and assisting ministers may greet people as they leave the service. They may assist the altar guild or other ministers in tidying up the communion vessels. With vestments and microphones returned to their places, the service is finished and everyone turns to the next items for their day: coffee hour or, in some cases, education hour, meetings, another service, or perhaps lunch with family or friends.

Your important work might be aided by a brief word with the presiding minister, noting what went well and where difficulties cropped up. If need be, a time can be set to discuss these issues further, perhaps when the worship planning team meets.

In all cases, a welcome conclusion to the service is grateful thanks for sharing in worship leadership together!

I give thanks to God for the journey through this handbook with you. Serving the assembly's prayer, you will participate in God's mission of mercy and love for all creation. Amen!

Summary of duties

Here is a general summary of tasks the assisting minister may encounter. Most congregations will have their own local variations and specific needs.

Before worship

- Recalling training, mentally rehearsing role as preparation for calm and confident presence
- Arriving early to rehearse, talk through logistics with presiding minister
- Putting on vestment and placing microphone
- Joining in prayer with worship leaders

Gathering

- Processing
- Holding the leaders book for confession and forgiveness or thanksgiving for baptism
- Helping with sprinkling, if used
- Leading Kyrie, canticle of praise, other gathering song
- Holding leaders book for greeting (if needed) and prayer of the day

Word

- If reading scripture, doing so with confidence and clarity
- If there is a gospel procession: carrying the Bible or lectionary

- Listening attentively to gospel and sermon; joining in singing the hymn of the day
- If praying the intercessions, checking that they have been prepared and placed in the leaders book
- Sharing peace, presiding minister first, then assembly

Meal
- Preparing the table
- Setting the table with bread and wine
- Receiving offering
- Praying offering prayer
- Assisting presider throughout the great thanksgiving
- Distributing bread or wine as directed by presiding minister
- Returning unused bread and wine to credence (side) table
- Praying prayer after communion

Sending
- Holding leaders book for the blessing (if needed)
- Speaking the dismissal

After worship
- Greeting departing worshipers
- Thanking other worship leaders and the presiding minister
- Cleaning up remaining communion vessels
- Returning alb and microphone

Preparing the prayers of intercession

Martin Luther offered excellent advice on Christian prayer in the little pamphlet, *A Simple Way to Pray*, written at the request of Master Peter, his barber. Among other things, Luther suggested if a prayer is so generic that we can't remember it afterward, we may as well have just babbled heavenward. Rather, he suggests, even when meditating on a prayer as familiar as the Lord's Prayer, we ought to pause after each petition and add in the daily concerns of our heart, congregation, and town.

In what follows, I offer some thoughts about preparing and leading the prayers of intercession. Further materials to help you are included in *Leading Worship Matters: A Sourcebook for Preparing Worship Leaders* (Minneapolis: Augsburg Fortress, 2013).

First, either on your own or, better, in conversation with others, study the appointed lectionary texts. A complete list of the scripture texts assigned for each Sunday in the three-year lectionary cycle is printed in *Evangelical Lutheran Worship*, pages 18–63. Identify major themes and imagery from scripture for use in the prayers. If possible, find out what direction the preacher will take with the scriptures in the sermon, and what hymns will be sung. The prayers fit into an overall pattern of weaving the word into worship—in prayer, song, and proclamation.

> The prayers are prepared locally for each occasion.
> (*Evangelical Lutheran Worship*, p. 105)

The prayers are an integral part of worship and should be prepared with much thought, time, care, and personal prayer. As you craft petitions, keep in mind there is an overall arc and several general prayer categories to consider as a checklist. The pattern includes a bid or petition related to a general topic, concluding with a call and response inviting assembly participation and assent such as: Lord, in your mercy, / **hear our prayer**. Prayers reflect the wideness of God's mercy for the whole world:

- **for the church universal, its ministry, and the mission of the gospel**—for all the baptized, bishops and pastors of the church, other leaders, missionaries, preaching and teaching, church schools, the unity of Christians;

- **for the well-being of creation**—care of the earth and sea, harvest, the whole environment, the cosmos;

- **for peace and justice in the world, the nations and those in authority, the community**—for leaders of government and international organizations, regions and/or people experiencing natural, political, or economic crises, elections, promotions of justice and peace;

- **for the poor, oppressed, sick, bereaved, lonely**—those who are poor, homeless, unemployed, lonely, exiles and refugees, sick, dying, prisoners, persecuted for the faith;

- **for all who suffer in body, mind, or spirit**—and especially those we know by name;

- **for the congregation, for local and specific concerns**—city, neighborhood, and seminary issues, musicians, artists, other worship leaders, staff, visitors, guests, upcoming events, hardships facing the community;

- **thanksgiving for the faithful departed**—members of the congregation, those close to the community, relatives who have recently died, those commemorated on the church's calendar.

When reflecting on these seven general categories, it can be helpful to **consider the liturgical day and season**, the texts for the day, and other liturgical texts that may be appointed for the day. For example, the intercessions written for Lent (a time of baptismal preparation) would be distinguished from those written for Advent (a time for welcoming the light); Pentecost Sunday would be distinct from Christ the King; and so on.

From season to season, a certain variety may be present in language, responses, and needs that are voiced. While they may reflect cultural as well as global concerns, they ought not be so specific that a particular assembly could not understand or respond to the bid. Prayer writers need to **be aware of the social, cultural, and economic diversity of the community** on whose behalf the prayers are being offered.

Avoid political slant to either the right or left. On the one hand, we need not avoid the very particular issues facing our community, nation, and world. On the other hand, prayers are not speeches. We pray to God with openness to God's wisdom and work in the world. At times, our faith may compel us to pray in ways some may interpret as partisan or political, such as following our Lord's command to love our enemies and pray for those who persecute us (Matthew 5:44).

In his little book *When You Pray*, theologian Douglas John Hall worries that prayer in North America too easily becomes another tool for self-cultivation—with "a view to becoming more fulfilled, acceptable, interesting, beautiful, psychically stable, integrated, irenic, healthy, happy, satisfied, or positive people" (Wipf and Stock, 2003, p. 12). Locally written prayers of intercession might open the door to half-baked theology of just this sort. When we pray, we are certainly not lifting our hopes for personal or national self-improvement or safety skyward. Rather, the whole biblical witness shows us a God who comes near, who hears our cries, and who seeks to work healing, reconciliation, and renewal for all creation.

The prayers of intercession are neither exhortations nor confessions. **Aim for petitions that are succinct but not terse.** Fewer words can open the prayer more widely to the assembly's participation; piles of words can limit this participation.

Avoid preachy prayers—that is, petitions that get too long and try to manipulate people's behavior. The prayers of intercession are not a second sermon. To avoid a preachy tone, you might use this simple formula:

> For the whole church on earth . . .
> For the people of God in *name of country* . . .
> For (*whatever else you want to include in the prayers*) . . .

This formula avoids saying what, exactly, is hoped as an outcome of the prayer and thus avoids setting out a social, political, or finger-wagging agenda.

As the prayer of a gathered community, **petitions are regularly voiced in the first person plural** (we/us). This may seem obvious, but it underlines the corporate character of the prayers. They are the prayers of the whole gathered assembly, not of an individual.

The prayers of intercession are generally addressed to God, the first person of the Trinity. In their form, the prayers of intercession echo the bidding prayers voiced in the Good Friday liturgy. The bidding prayers are the prayers of the people as they look upon the suffering Christ. The suffering in the world is Christ's suffering. The prayers are a plea to God the Creator. Other attributes or names for God may be used, for example:

Hear us, merciful God.

Reveal your saving power.

Hear us, shepherd of Israel.

The petitions may be **addressed directly to God**:

Send your blessing upon seedtime and harvest, the commerce and industry of your people. Give them just rewards for their labor and protect them from all danger. Hear us, merciful God.

Or the intercessor may first **address the assembly**:

Let us pray for the holy church of God throughout the world, for its leaders and ministers, that God will guide it and preserve it. (*Pause*) Hear us, O God.

When preparing intercessions, take care that the petitions are addressed either to God or to the assembly, not moving back and forth.

The petition for those in need will usually allow for the naming of the sick or dying and for other intentions:

> Let us pray for those who are sick or recovering from illness, (*especially*).

Likewise, when an intercession is offered for people or regions in crisis, or a thanksgiving for the faithful departed, you may allow time for the assembly to name specific people or places:

> Let us pray for those experiencing hardship or distress around the world. For whom do we pray? (*Pause for assembly's intercessions.*)

> Let us pray in thanksgiving for those who loved and served God in the church who now rest from their labors. Especially we give thanks for . . . (*pause for assembly's thanksgivings*).

The assembly's response to each petition may be either in the form of a plea (God, in your mercy, / **hear our prayer**.) or in the form of a thanksgiving (Bless we the Lord. / **Thanks be to God**.). Other responses may also be used.

It is a helpful practice to find an editorial partner who will regularly review and respond to the prayers you prepare, thinking about issues discussed above as well as the basic principles of writing for the ear. Like other prayers, the prayers of intercession are to be spoken aloud, heard, and prayed from the heart by the assembly. Either with this partner or alone, read the prayers out loud to yourself to make sure they feel smooth to you and fit easily on your tongue. Be alert for words that sound the same but are spelled differently, and how they may be heard by the assembly (for example, *reign* and *rain*).

In tone, prayers should be neither too pedestrian (as if you are speaking to someone at coffee hour) nor too pious (in flowery, "religious" language you would normally never use). It matters that the person praying seems natural, seems himself or herself. Your natural ease both in word and embodied action invites and allows the assembly to join in, with, and through your leadership as together you pray earnestly to God for all the world.

Preparing for worship

Romans 12:1-8

I appeal to you therefore, brothers and sisters, by the mercies of God, to present your bodies as a living sacrifice, holy and acceptable to God, which is your spiritual worship. Do not be conformed to this world, but be transformed by the renewing of your minds, so that you may discern what is the will of God—what is good and acceptable and perfect.

For by the grace given to me I say to everyone among you not to think of yourself more highly than you ought to think, but to think with sober judgment, each according to the measure of faith that God has assigned. For as in one body we have many members, and not all the members have the same function, so we, who are many, are one body in Christ, and individually we are members one of another. We have gifts that differ according to the grace given to us: prophecy, in proportion to faith; ministry, in ministering; the teacher, in teaching; the exhorter, in exhortation; the giver, in generosity; the leader, in diligence; the compassionate, in cheerfulness.

Spirit of the living God, you have called us here to this place for worship and praise. Move powerfully, calling from each the gifts we have to offer. Bless our leadership so we might show forth your love, giving ourselves away as servants of your people. May we come with open hands and hearts, expecting your mercy to lead us, and your love to support us. In Jesus' name. Amen.

or

Holy God, I thank you for calling me to serve as an assisting minister. I ask your blessing that as I prepare to assist in the ministry of word and table, I may do so with dignity and grace, and all to your glory, and for the welfare of your people. Amen.

For further reading

Brugh, Lorraine S., and Gordon W. Lathrop. *The Sunday Assembly*: Using Evangelical Lutheran Worship, vol 1. Minneapolis: Augsburg Fortress, 2008. A resource to guide leaders in their understanding and interpretation of *Evangelical Lutheran Worship* resources. Focuses on holy communion.

Eastwood, Cyril. *The Priesthood of All Believers: An Examination of the Doctrine from the Reformation to the Present Day.* London: The Epworth Press, 1960. The standard work on the recovery of the proper leadership role of the laity in worship, paving the way for a recovery of the assisting minister role in Protestant churches and the deaconate in its various forms across the churches.

Hall, Douglas John. *When You Pray: Thinking Your Way into God's World.* Eugene, OR: Wipf and Stock, 2003. A major North American theologian speaks about the challenges of prayer today.

Hoyer, Christopher George. *Getting the Word Out: A Handbook for Readers*. Minneapolis: Augsburg Fortress, 2013. Practical helps and spiritual wisdom for those who serve as readers in the assembly.

Lathrop, Gordon W. *Central Things: Worship in Word and Sacrament*. Minneapolis: Augsburg Fortress, 2005. One of the Worship Matters Studies. This concise book considers what worship in word and sacrament really is and why it matters so much.

Leading Worship Matters: A Sourcebook for Preparing Worship Leaders. Multiple contributors. Minneapolis: Augsburg Fortress, 2013. Practical, succinct, easy-to-use tools and resources to plan, execute, and evaluate worship leadership training. Covers assisting ministers, readers, intercessors, acolytes, ushers, greeters, communion ministers, altar guild, tech ministers, musicians and cantors, and more. Includes companion DVD.

Luther, Martin. *A Simple Way to Pray*. Translated by Matthew C. Harrison. Louisville: Westminster John Knox, 2011. In response to a question from his barber, Master Peter, Martin Luther offers thoughtful and approachable advice on prayer.

Sloyan, Virgina. *Touchstones for Liturgical Ministers* Collegeville, MN: Liturgical Press, 1978. An excellent booklet composed of a set of brief essays on leadership in assembly.

Stauffer, S. Anita. *Altar Guild and Sacristy Handbook*, 4th rev. ed. Minneapolis: Augsburg Fortress, 2014. Revised edition of this classic on preparing the table and the worship environment.

Sundays and Seasons. Multiple contributors. Minneapolis: Augsburg Fortress, annual. A guide to worship planning with reflections on the lectionary readings, sample prayers of intercession, and other helps for weekly worship preparation.

Van Loon, Ralph R. *Assisting Ministers Handbook.* S. Anita Stauffer, ed. Philadelphia: Parish Life Press, 1990. A resource developed for introduction of *Lutheran Book of Worship* with extensive discussion of each part of the liturgy, a study guide, and a helpful bibliography.

Wengert, Timothy J., ed. *Centripetal Worship: The Evangelical Heart of Lutheran Worship.* Minneapolis: Augsburg Fortress, 2007. One of the Worship Matters Studies. Contributors look at the historical and contemporary factors that influence how and why we worship the way we do.

Worship Matters: An Introduction to Worship. Multiple contributors. Minneapolis: Augsburg Fortress, 2012. Illuminates the whys and hows of Christian worship so that worshipers might experience a deeper appreciation of their community's worship. Leader guide also available.